ENGLISH

1st Grade
Age 3 -7

Copyright © 2022 by Kireeha S. Plair

Copyright © 2022 by Kireeha S. Plair

This is a work of creative nonfiction.

All rights reserved. No part of this book may be reproduced or used in any manner without written permission of the copyright owner except for the use of quotations in a book review.

First paperback edition

Book design by Kireeha S. Plair

ISBN: 978-1-7368783-3-0

Published by: Literature Rays

Email: Literaturerays80@aol.com

ENGLISH ACTIVITY BOOK

CONTENTS

- Letters of the Alphabet
- The Lowercase Alphabet
- The Uppercase Alphabet
- Alphabet Upper case Letter Tracing
- Vowels and Consonant Sounds
- Short Vowel Sounds (a, e, o, i, u)
- Singular and Plural Words
- Reading Print (e.g. from left to right, top to bottom)
- Rhyming Words
- First, Next, Last (e.g. The Story is out of order
- Noun, Verbs and Adjectives
- Question words (e.g. who, what, where, when, why, how)
- The parts of the body
- Labels (e.g. write labels naming the parts of the body)

Hi, I'm Kaleb let's have some English fun!

The Alphabet

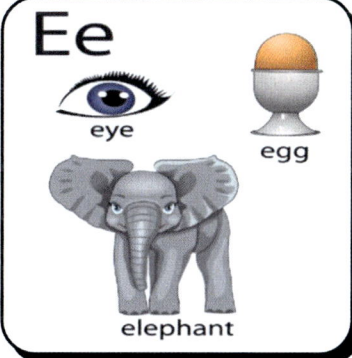

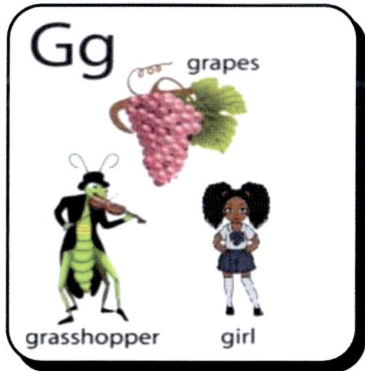

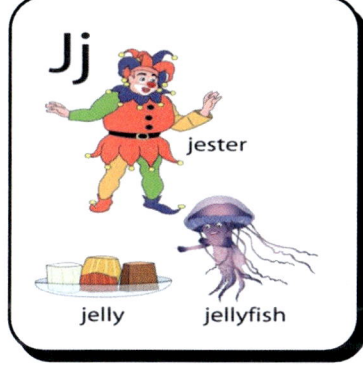

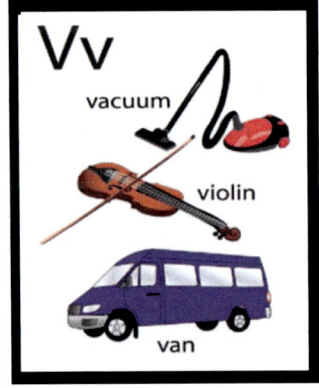

Upper and Lower Case Alphabet

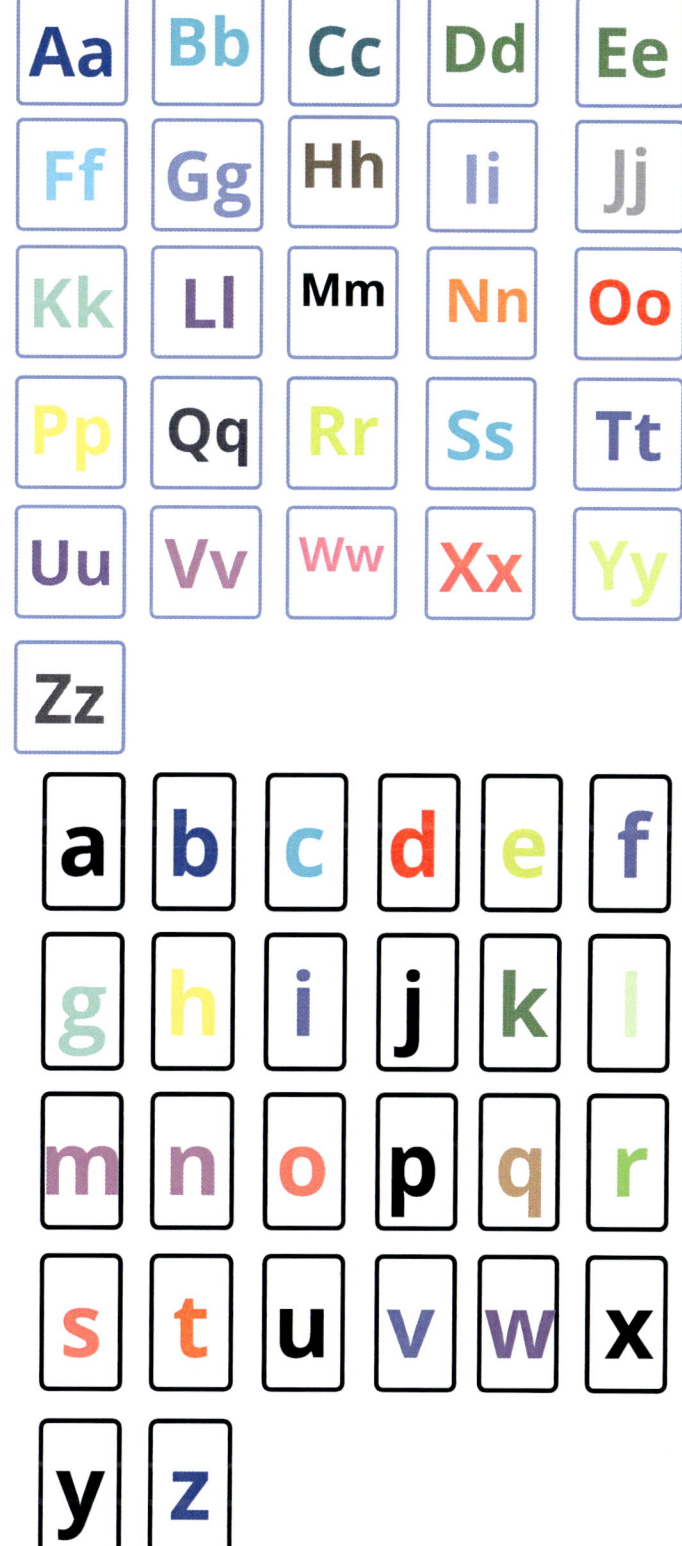

A	A	A	A	A	N	N	N	N
B	B	B	B	B	O	O	O	O
C	C	C	C	C	P	P	P	P
D	D	D	D	D	Q	Q	Q	Q
E	E	E	E	E	R	R	R	R
F	F	F	F	F	S	S	S	S
G	G	G	G	G	T	T	T	T
H	H	H	H	H	U	U	U	U
I	I	I	I	I	V	V	V	V
J	J	J	J	J	W	W	W	W
K	K	K	K	K	X	X	X	X
L	L	L	L	L	Y	Y	Y	Y
M	M	M	M	M	Z	Z	Z	Z

a_____ b_____ c_____ d_____

e_____ f_____ g_____ h_____

i_____ j_____ k_____ l_____

m_____   n_____

o_____ p_____ q_____ r_____

s_____ t_____ u_____ v_____

w_____ x_____ y_____ z_____

Sorting Constants and Vowels

Q. Short the following letters

1. a,c,e,h

Constants	Vowels

2. i,k,t,u

Constants	Vowels

3. m,o,i,s

Constants	Vowels

4. e,h,i,j

Constants	Vowels

5. a,s,u,k

Constants	Vowels

6. u,x,a,f

Constants	Vowels

Vowels and Constants

How many vowels are in the following words.

baby **1**   apple ☐

puppy ☐   ball ☐

sweet ☐   smart ☐

elephant ☐   dinosaur ☐

lion ☐   hippoptamus ☐

Constant Sounds

b bb bat rabbit	c k ck ch q cat kite duck school queen	ch tch church watch	d dd drum ladder	f ff ph fish cliff phone
g gg girl egg	h hop	j g ge dge jelly giant cage bridge	l ll lolipop ball	m mm mb meal hammer lamb
n nn kn net dinner knee	ng n king ink	p pp pink slipper	r rr wr rip cherry wrist	s ss se c se snake kiss house city ice
sh ti ch shark station chef	t tt tennis letter	th th thumb feather	v ve van sleeve	w wh u wind whale queen
qu quack	y yoghurt	z zz ze s se zip buzz sneeze laser cheese	s si treasure television	x cks box rocks

Short Vowels

Short a

ab	ad	ag	am	an	ap	at
cab	bad	bag	bam	ban	cap	bat
dab	dad	gag	dam	can	gap	cat
gab	had	hag	ham	fan	tap	fat
jab	mad	lag	jam	man	map	hat
lab	pad	nag	ram	pan	nap	mat
nab	sad	rag	yam	ran	rap	pat
tab	tad	sag		tan	sap	rat
		tag		van	tap	sat
		wag			yap	vat
					zap	

Short e

ed	eg	en	et	
bed	beg	den	bet	web
fed	keg	hen	get	gem
led	leg	men	jet	hem
red	peg	pen	let	pep
wed		ten	met	yes
			net	
			pet	
			set	
			vet	
			wet	
			yet	

Short i

id	ig	im	in	ip	it	ix
bid	big	dim	bin	dip	bit	fix
did	dig	him	din	hip	fit	mix
hid	fig	rim	fin	lip	hit	six
kid	gig		pin	nip	kit	
lid	jig		sin	rip	lit	
rid	pig		tin	sip	pit	
	rig		win	tip	sit	
	wig			zip	wit	
	zig					

Short o

ob	og	op	ot	ox	
cob	bog	cop	cot	box	mom
gob	cog	hop	dot	fox	rod
job	dog	mop	got	pox	
lob	fog	pop	hot		
mob	hog	top	jot		
rob	jog		lot		
sob	log		not		
			pot		
			rot		
			tot		

Short u

ub	ud	ug	um	un	ut	
cub	bud	bug	bum	bun	but	cup
hub	cud	dug	gum	fun	cut	pup
nub	dud	hug	hum	gun	gut	bus
rub	mud	jug	mum	nun	hut	
sub		lug	sum	pun	jut	
tub		mug		run	nut	
		pug		sun	rut	
		rug				
		tug				

Plural Words

Plural means more than one. look at the pictures below an circle the correct word.

flag   flags   child   children

instrument   instruments   animal   animals

umbrella   umbrellas   ball   balls

Singular and Plural words

Singular means one. Plural means more than one. Look at the pictures. Complete the sentences with either the singular or plural word.

This is a _____

These are _____

This is a _____

These are _____

This is a _____

Singular and Plural words

Singular means one. Plural means more than one. Look at the pictures. Complete the sentences with either the singular or plural word.

This is a _____

These are _____

These are _____

This is a _____

This is a _____

Facing left or right

Is the bird facing left or right? Circle the correct answer.

left right	left right	left right
left right	left right	left right
left right	left right	left right
left right	left right	left right
left right	left right	left right
left right	left right	left right

Facing left or right

**Circle the animals facing <u>left</u>.
Draw a box around the animals facing <u>right</u>.**

Understanding "before" and "after"

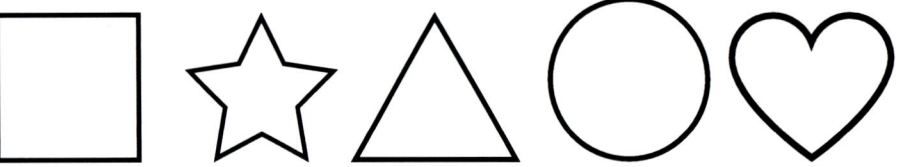

Color the shape **before** the triangle blue.

Color the shape **after** the triangle yellow.

Color the shape **before** the star green.

Color the shape **after** the circle red.

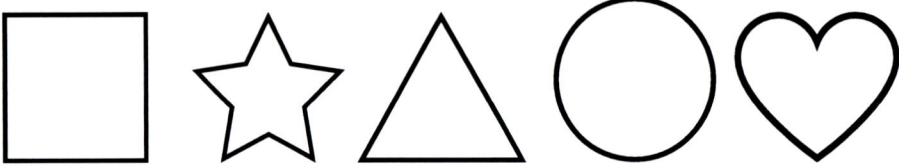

Color the shape **after** the star green.

Color the shape **before** the heart red.

Color the shape **after** the circle yellow.

Color the shape **before** the triangle blue.

Rhyming words - matching

Draw a line between the pictures that rhyme with each other.

Matching words that rhyme

Draw a line between the words that rhyme.

back	rat
cake	tank
bank	sack
jar	late
cat	bake
gate	far

Character and Setting

Draw a line from the picture to the word that describes if its a character or setting best.

Character

Setting

Character

Setting

Character

Setting

Character

Setting

What's the order

Put the pictures in order by writing 1, 2 or 3 below the picture.

_____   _____   _____

_____   _____   _____

_____   _____   _____

NOUN	VERB	ADJECTIVE	ADVERB
beauty	beautify	beautiful	beautyfully
benefit beneficiary	benefit	beneficial	beneficially
creation creator	create	creative	creatively
decision	decide	decisive	decisively
difference	differentiate	different	differently
distraction	distract	distracted distracting	distractedly
justification	justify	justifiable	justifiably
protection	protect	protective	protectively
reliability	rely	reliable	reliably
sadness	sadden	sad	sadly
significance	signify	significant	significantly
strength	strengthen	strong	strongly
success	succeed	successful	successfully
understanding	understand	understandable	understandably

ADJECTIVES

witch	angry	bike	sad
neat	beautiful	Tom	cried
tall	writing	loud	happy

NOUNS

car	red	Elim Road	cold
television	dog	pen	ran
shouted	rock	freezing	text book

VERBS

shouted	think	run	back
tidy	was	yellow	James
write	after	skipped	ran

Sorting Nouns and Verbs

Write the nouns and verbs in the correct box

NOUNS	VERBS

turkey	cooked	corn	bread	pie	eating
dinner	playing	laughed	driving	salad	potato

- Circle the words that are **nouns**.

Cow	long	Red
tell	Book	read
pen	thin	Iran

- Circle the words that are **Adjectives**.

Loud	long	Red
tell	Book	read
Funny	thin	Far

- Circle the words that are **Verbs**.

play	long	taste
tell	Book	read
funny	look	Far

Classroom instructions

Question Words

What ?
It's used to ask about specific things, people, animals, and objects.

Which ?
It's used to ask about choices, and alternatives.

Where ?
It's used to ask about places, and positions.

Who?
It's used to ask about people, or a person.

When ?
It's used to ask about times, occasions, and moments.

Whose ?
It's used to ask about who's the possessor of something.

why ?
It's used to ask about reasons, and explanations.

How ?
It's used to show the way things work.

Question words

Read the question words. Draw a line from the question word to complete each sentence.

Who   deep is the lake?

When   time is it?

What   did this?

How   can we eat?

Question words

Read the question words. Draw a line from the question word to complete each sentence.

Where   will you leave?

Why   are they doing?

When   are you busy today?

What   is your hat?

Writing question words

Read the question words. write the question words to complete each question.

| where | why | how | who |

_____ are you crying?

_____ broke the toy?

_____ do you feel today?

_____ are you going?

MY BODY PARTS

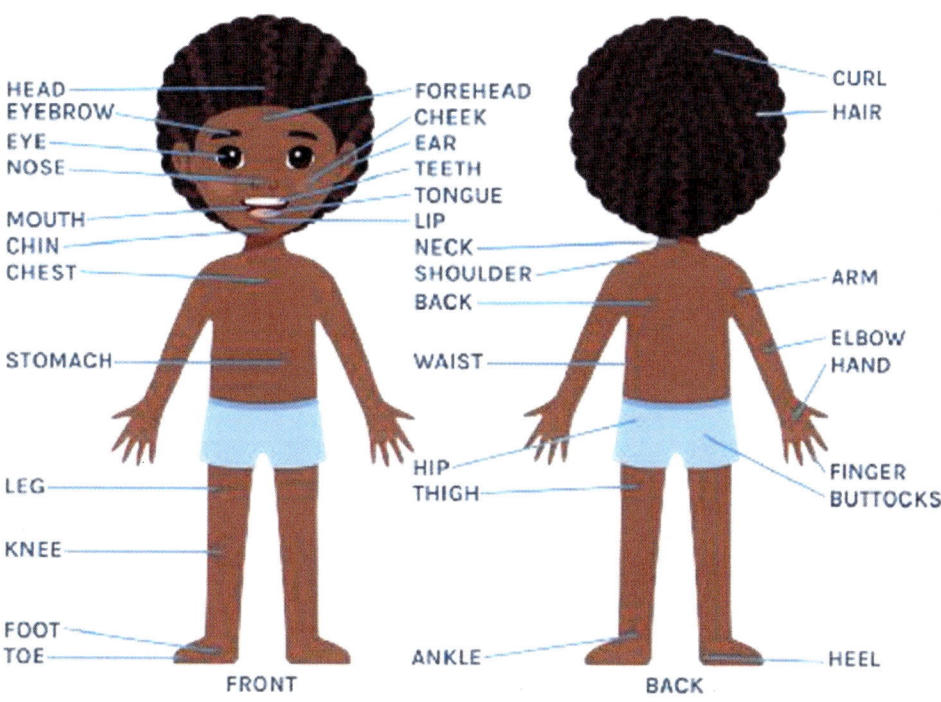

Writes the number that corresponds to each body part.

1.Hair 2.Head 3.Face 4.Neck 5.Chest 6.Arm
7.Stomach 8.Leg 9.Foot 10.Eye 11.Ear 12.Nose
13.Teeth 14.Mouth 15.Shoulder 16.Elbow
17.Finger 18.Knee 19.Toe 20.Hand

MATH ACTIVITY BOOK

CONTENTS

- **Counting and Tracing Whole Numbers (0-20)**
- **Whole Number Operations**
- **Relationship Between Numbers**
- **Cardinality (Counting Sets)**
- **Non-numerical Patterns**
- **Numerical Patterns**
- **Different Shapes**
- **Presentation of Data**
- **Addition of Numbers**
- **Subtraction of Numbers**

It's math time! 123 count with me

Trace the numbers

1 •	1 1 1 1 1 1 1
2 ••	2 2 2 2 2 2
3 •••	3 3 3 3 3 3
4 ••••	4 4 4 4 4 4
5 •••••	5 5 5 5 5 5
6 •••••	6 6 6 6 6 6
7 •••••••	7 7 7 7 7 7
8 ••••••••	8 8 8 8 8 8
9 •••••••••	9 9 9 9 9 9
10 ••••••••••	10 10 10 10 10

KINDERGARTEN ENGLISH & MATH ACTIVITY BOOK

11 ▦	11 11 11 11 11
12 ▦	12 12 12 12 12
13 ▦	13 13 13 13 13
14 ▦	14 14 14 14 14
15 ▦	15 15 15 15 15
16 ▦	16 16 16 16 16
17 ▦	17 17 17 17 17
18 ▦	18 18 18 18 18
19 ▦	19 19 19 19 19
20 ▦	20 20 20 20 20

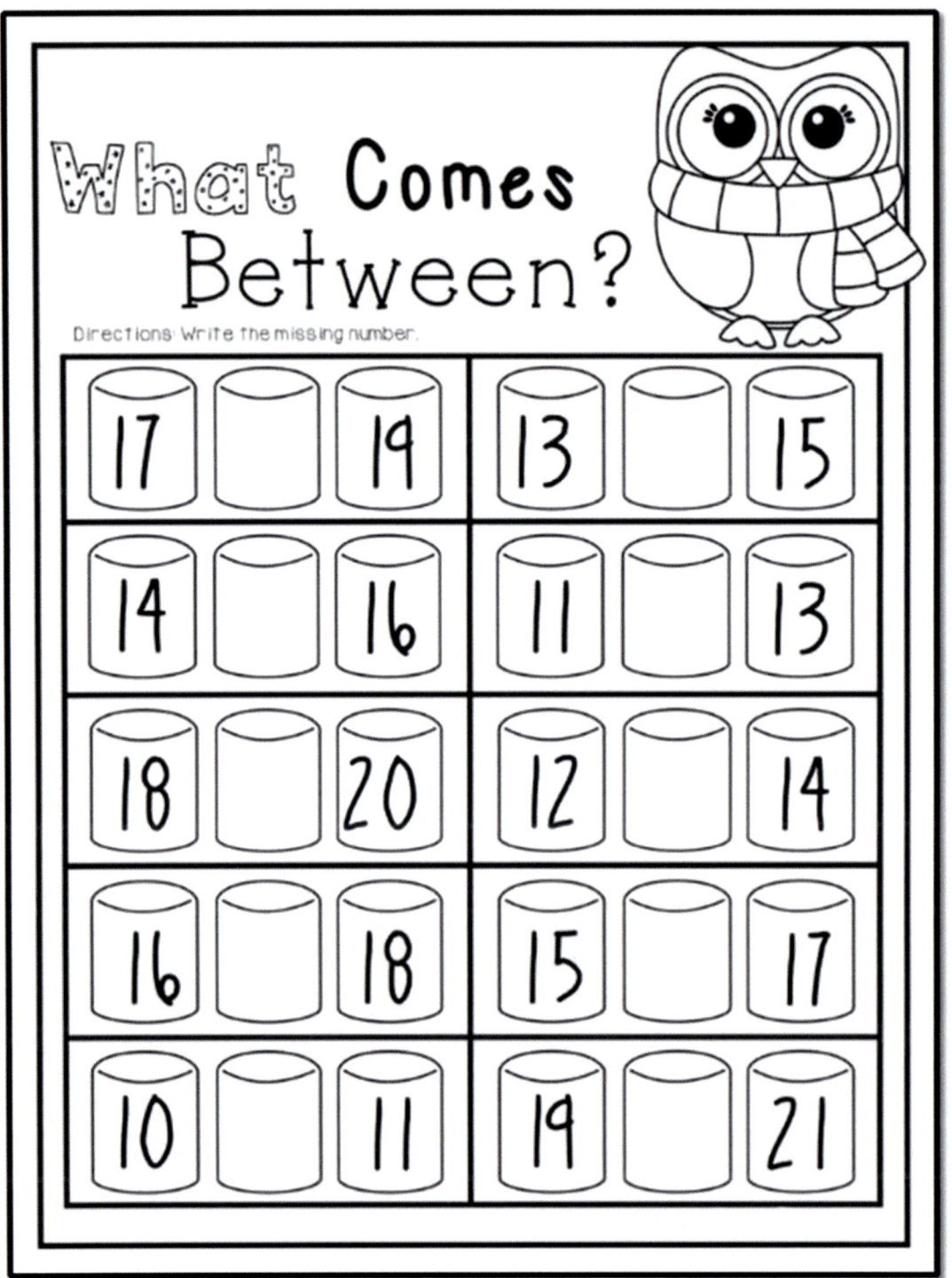

Comparing Number

Compare the numbers by adding > or > or =

1. 5 _ 3
2. 18 _ 1
3. 11 _ 14
4. 14 _ 17
5. 11 _ 14
6. 9 _ 16
7. 19 _ 16
8. 13 _ 10
9. 18 _ 8
10. 2 _ 5
11. 8 _ 3
12. 10 _ 18
13. 6 _ 7
14. 6 _ 18
15. 5 _ 15
16. 2 _ 6
17. 5 _ 1
18. 10 _ 6
19. 2 _ 12
20. 6 _ 6
21. 12 _ 11
22. 2 _ 17

Comparing numbers up to 10

 < = >

3 ☐ 6	4 ☐ 2
5 ☐ 8	1 ☐ 7
10 ☐ 9	3 ☐ 4
7 ☐ 2	5 ☐ 3
1 ☐ 9	8 ☐ 6

COUNTING FRUITS

Count the number of each fruits and write the answer in the circles given below,

Look at the pattern in each row. Circle the picture that continues the pattern. Color the pictures.

| 1 | 2 | 3 | 4 | 5 | 6 | 7 | 8 | 9 | 10 | 11 | 12 | 13 | 14 | 15 |

Can you help **Kaleb** to fill in the missing numbers by counting *on* in ones.

1)

| 4 | 5 | 6 | | 8 | 9 | | 11 |

2)

| 5 | | 7 | 8 | | 10 | | 12 |

3)

| 7 | 8 | | 10 | 11 | | 13 | |

4)

| 6 | | 8 | 9 | | 11 | | 13 |

5)

| 8 | 9 | 10 | | 12 | | 14 | |

6)

| 6 | 7 | | | 10 | 11 | | 13 |

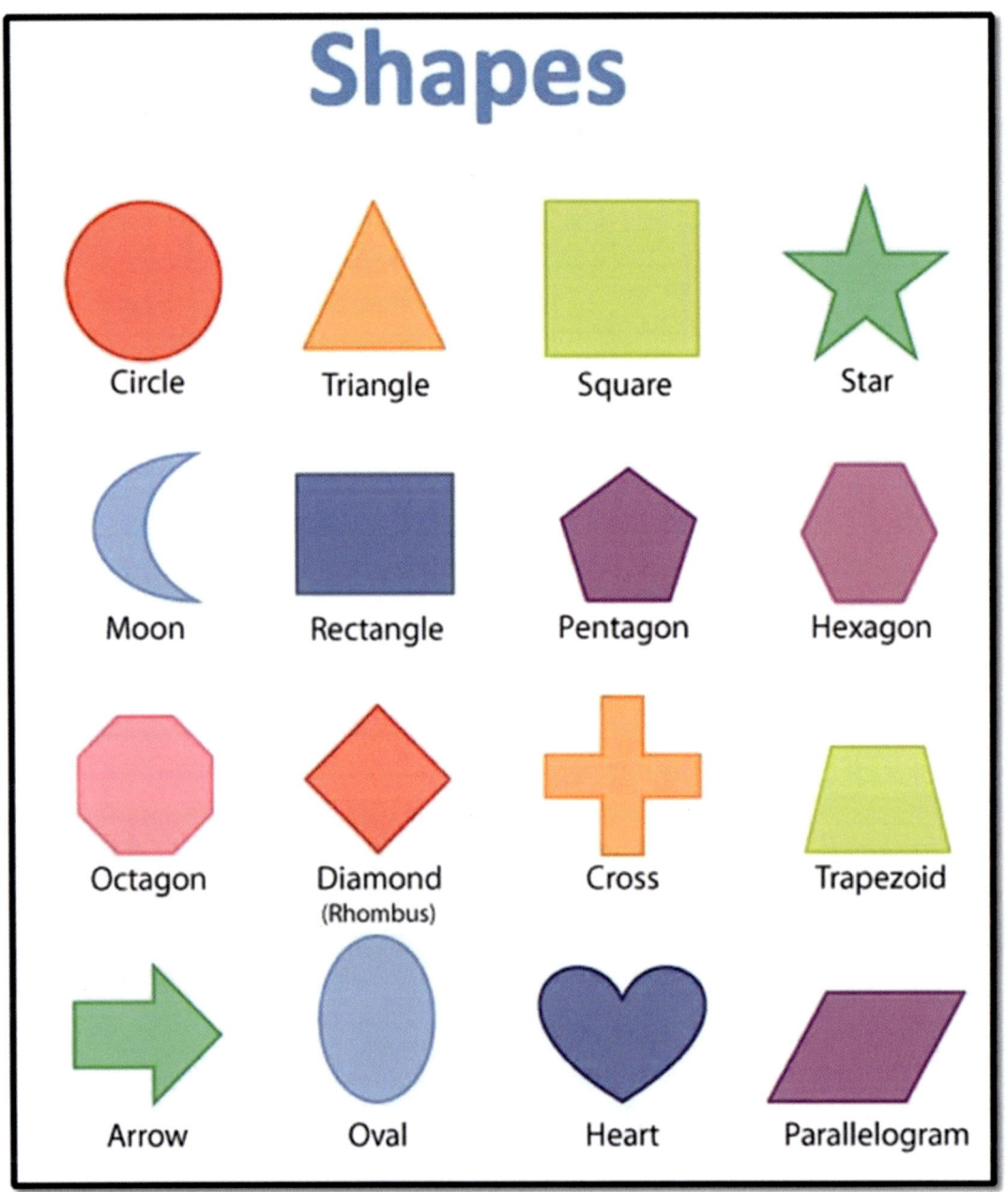

Draw lines from the real-world items to their matching shapes

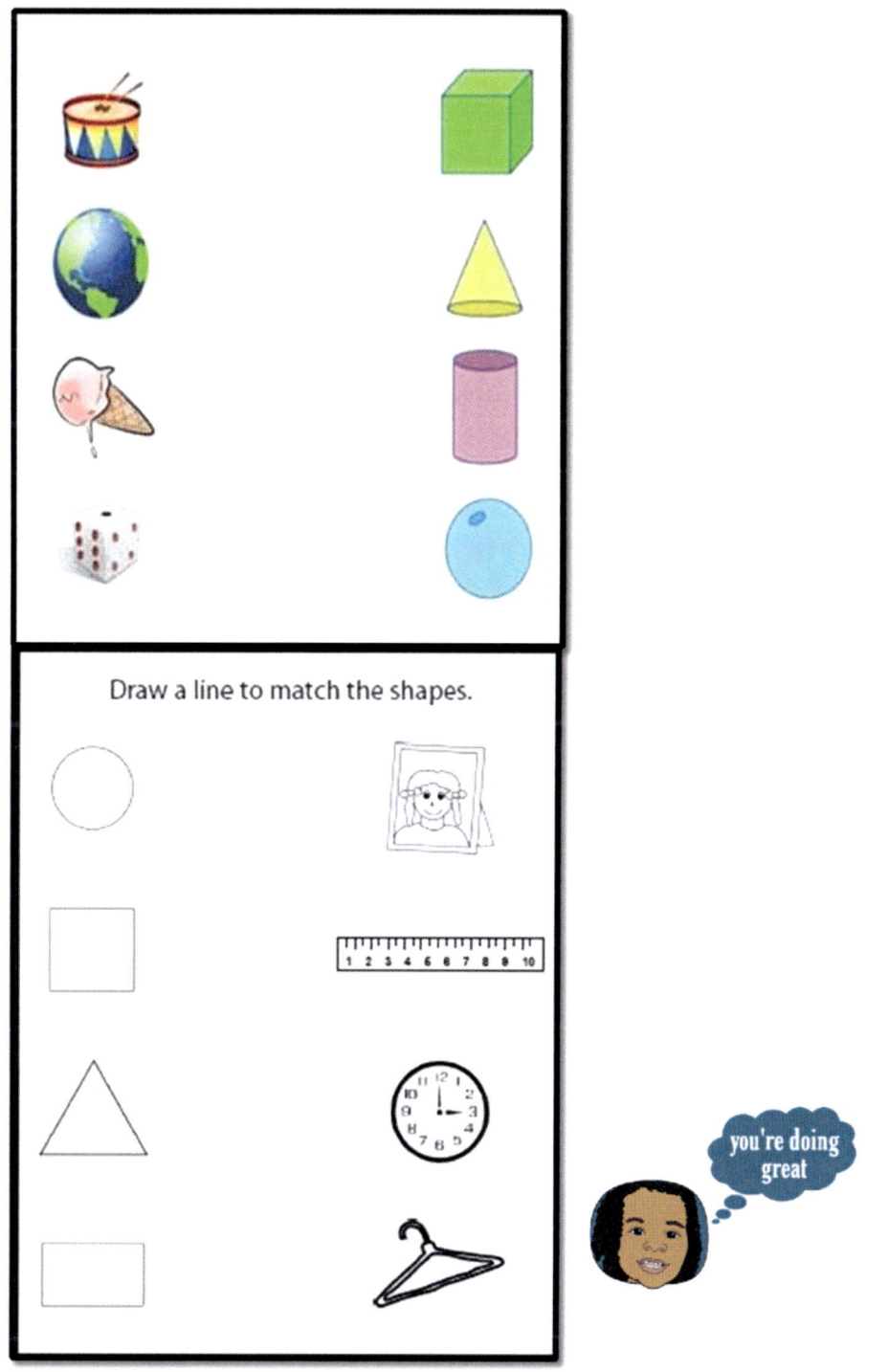

Measuring Length

Write the correct length.

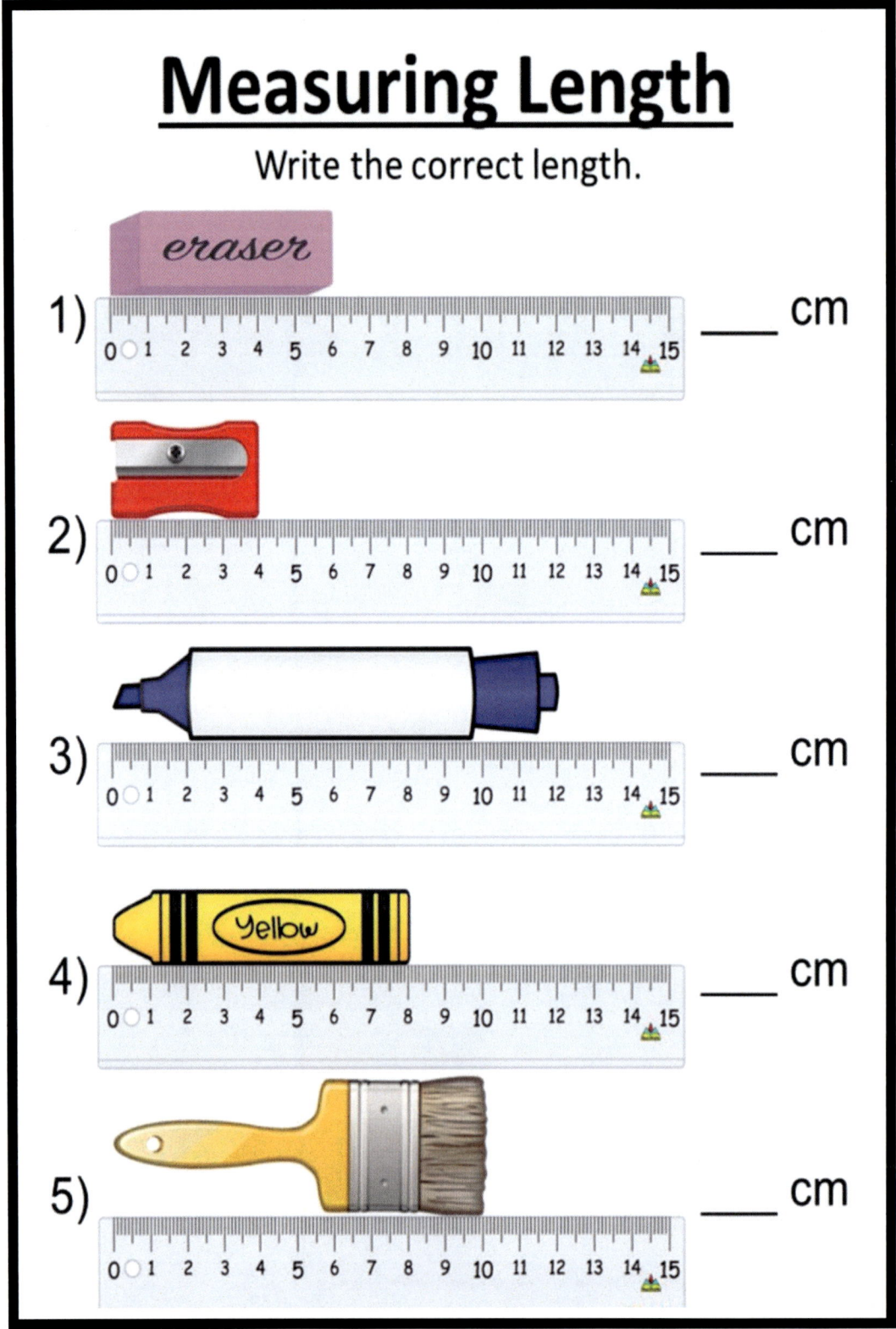

1) ____ cm

2) ____ cm

3) ____ cm

4) ____ cm

5) ____ cm

Math
Addition

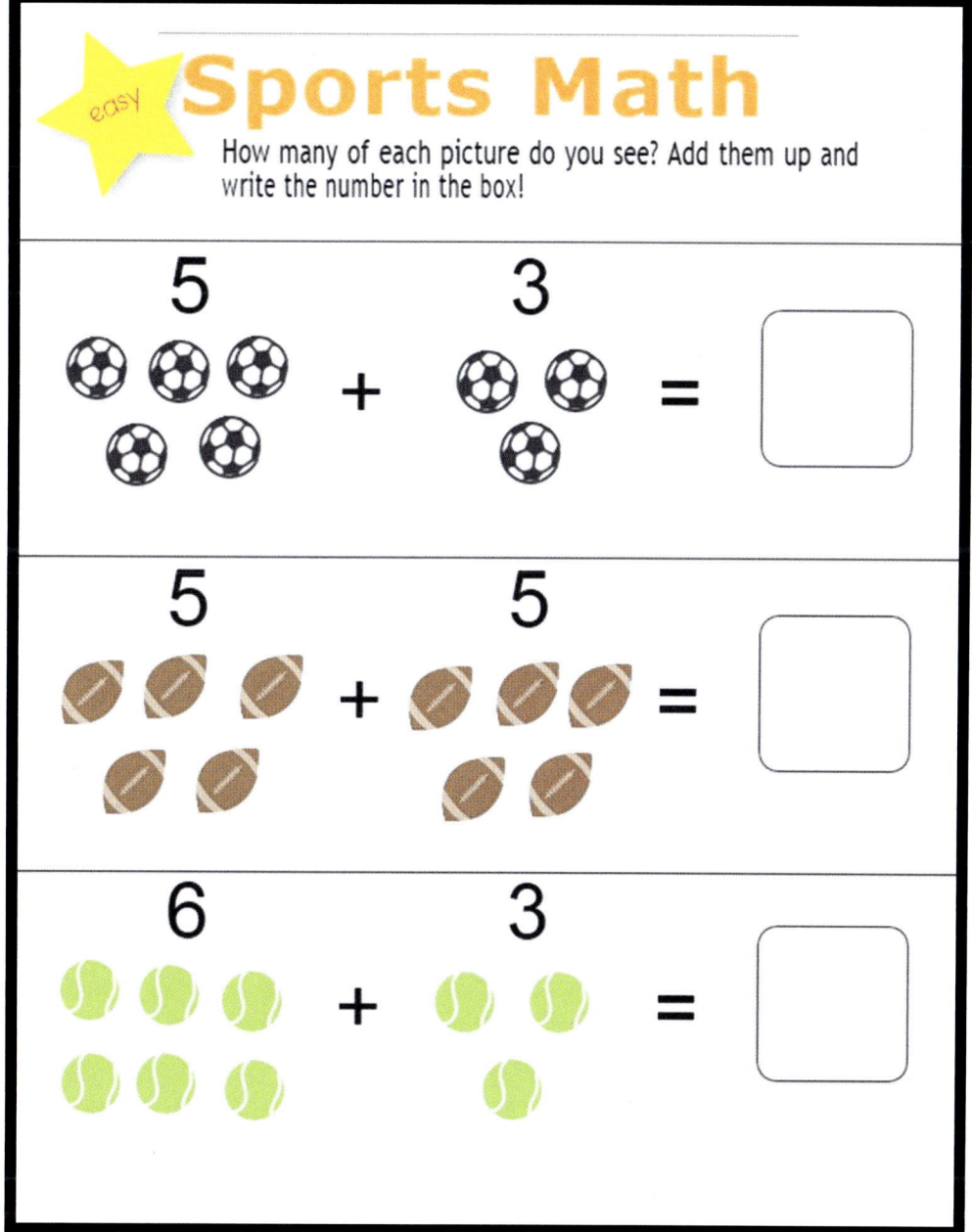

Adding Balloons: Up to 10!

Solve the addition problems below!

1. 4
   + 2
   ___

2. 6
   + 1
   ___

3. 5
   + 2
   ___

4. 3
   + 3
   ___

5. 4
   + 0
   ___

6. 5
   + 4
   ___

7. 6
   + 3
   ___

8. 7
   + 3
   ___

Keep going

PIRATE MATH

AHOY! I'm Pirate Billy. Will you help me count up my treasure? It's easy! How many of each picture do you see? Add them up and write the number in the box.

3 + 1 = ☐   4 + 2 = ☐

5 + 3 = ☐   5 + 4 = ☐

8 + 2 = ☐   4 + 3 = ☐

6 + 4 = ☐   5 + 5 = ☐

Fairy Addition

Add together the numbers below
and write down how many there are!

```
  2          2          3          4
+ 2        + 3        + 4        + 1
___        ___        ___        ___
```

2 + 3 = _____   3 + 2 = _____

4 + 1 = _____   3 + 4 = _____

How many fairies are there all together?

 +  = _____

Veggies Addition +

Add together the vegetables that are in each box and write your answer in the box on the right.

1. 🌟 🥬🥬 **+** 🥬🥬🥬   2
                                               +3
                                               ———

2. 🌟 radish radish radish radish **+** radish radish radish   4
       +3
   ———

3. 🌟 🥒🥒🥒 **+** 🥒🥒🥒   +3
   ———

4. 🌟 onion **+** onion onion onion onion onion   1
   +5
   ———

Garden Math

How many of each picture do you see? Add them up and write the number in the box!

4 + 4 =

5 + 1 =

2 + 5 =

Well done

KINDERGARTEN ENGLISH & MATH ACTIVITY BOOK

Fruity Addition +

Add together the fruits that are in each box and write your answer in the box on the right.

1. 🍌🍌🍌🍌 + 🍌🍌 | 4 +2

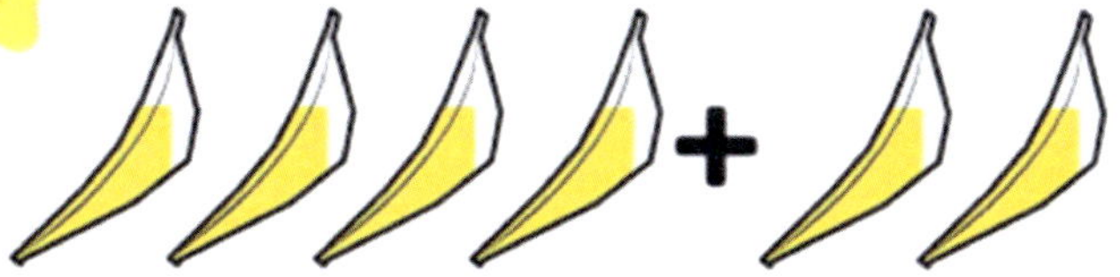

2. 🍒🍒🍒🍒🍒 + 🍒 | 5 +1

3. 🍍🍍🍍 + 🍍🍍🍍 | 3 +3

4. 🍉🍉 + 🍉🍉🍉 | 2 +3

Excellent work

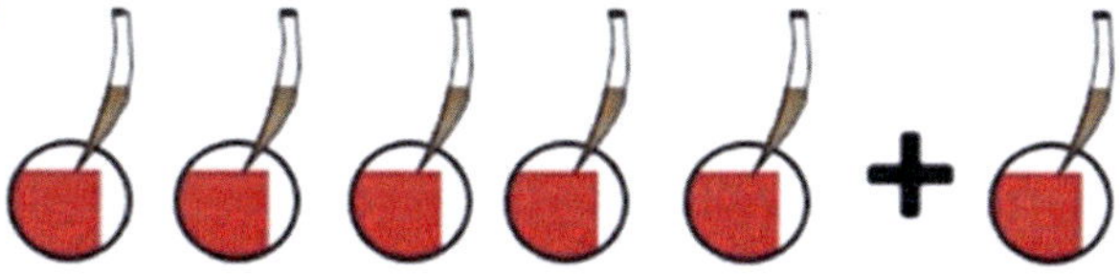

KINDERGARTEN ENGLISH & MATH ACTIVITY BOOK

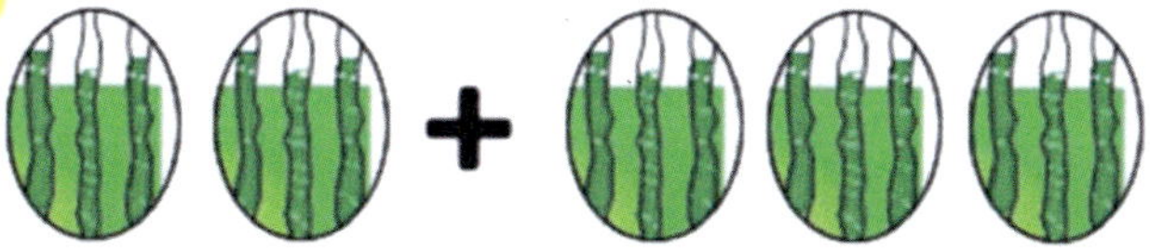

Math Subtraction

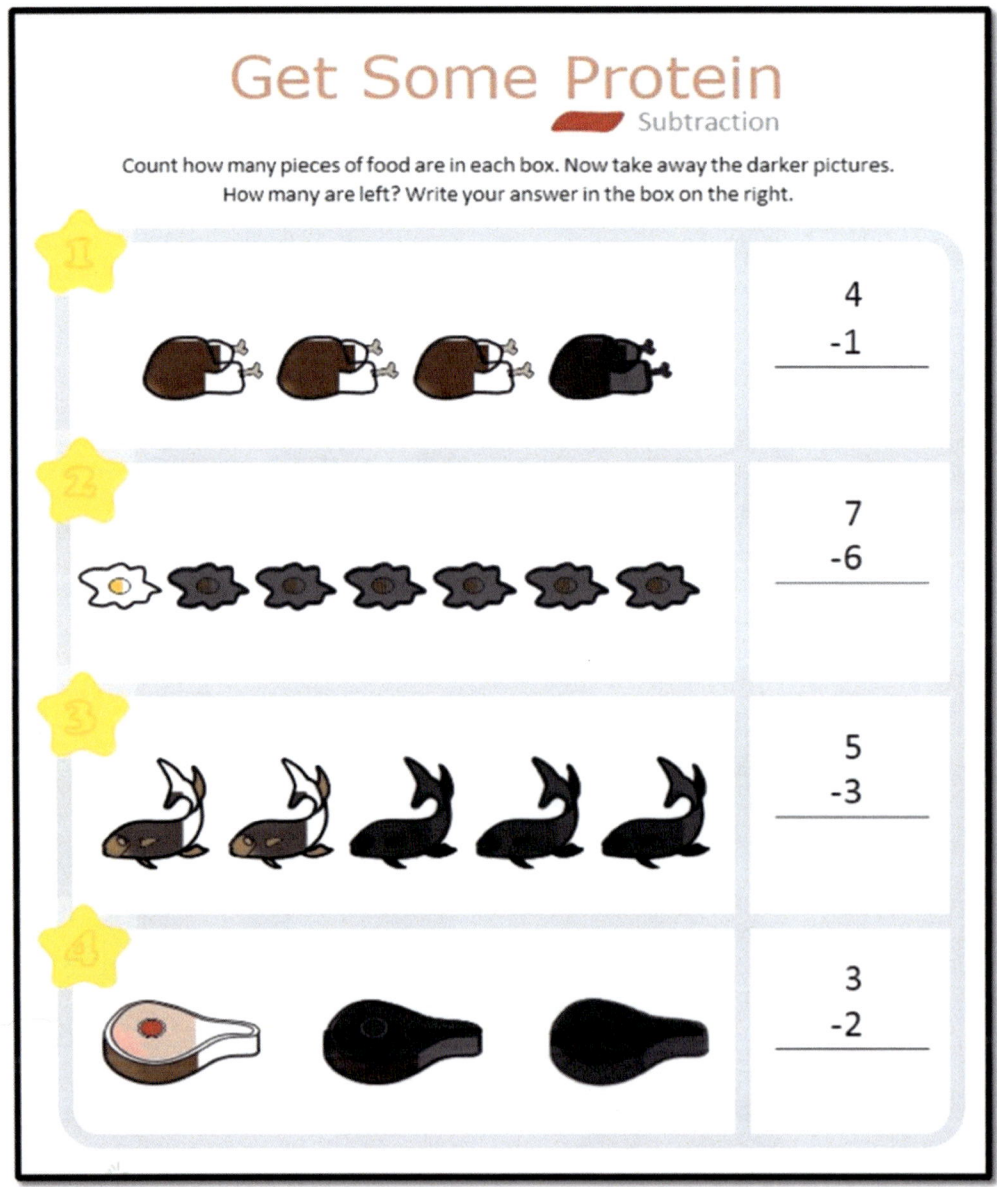

Falling Apples

Count the apples that have fallen from the tree.
Count how many apples are eaten.
Subtract to tell how many are left.

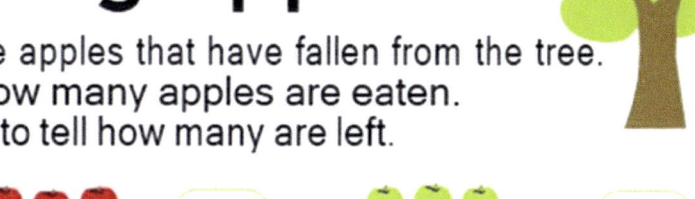

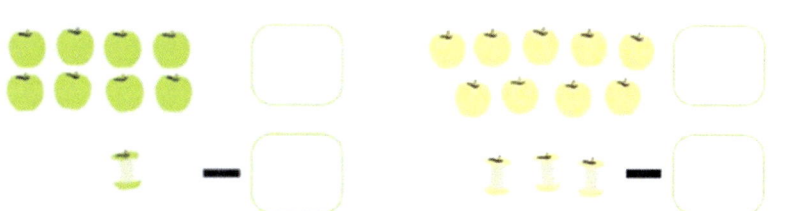

Mouse Snack

Count the pieces of cheese.
Count how many pieces the mouse eats.
Subtract to tell how many are left.

☐ − ☐ = ☐

☐ − ☐ = ☐

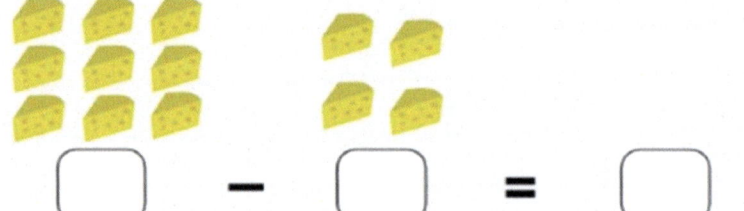

☐ − ☐ = ☐

☐ − ☐ = ☐

Subtraction to 10

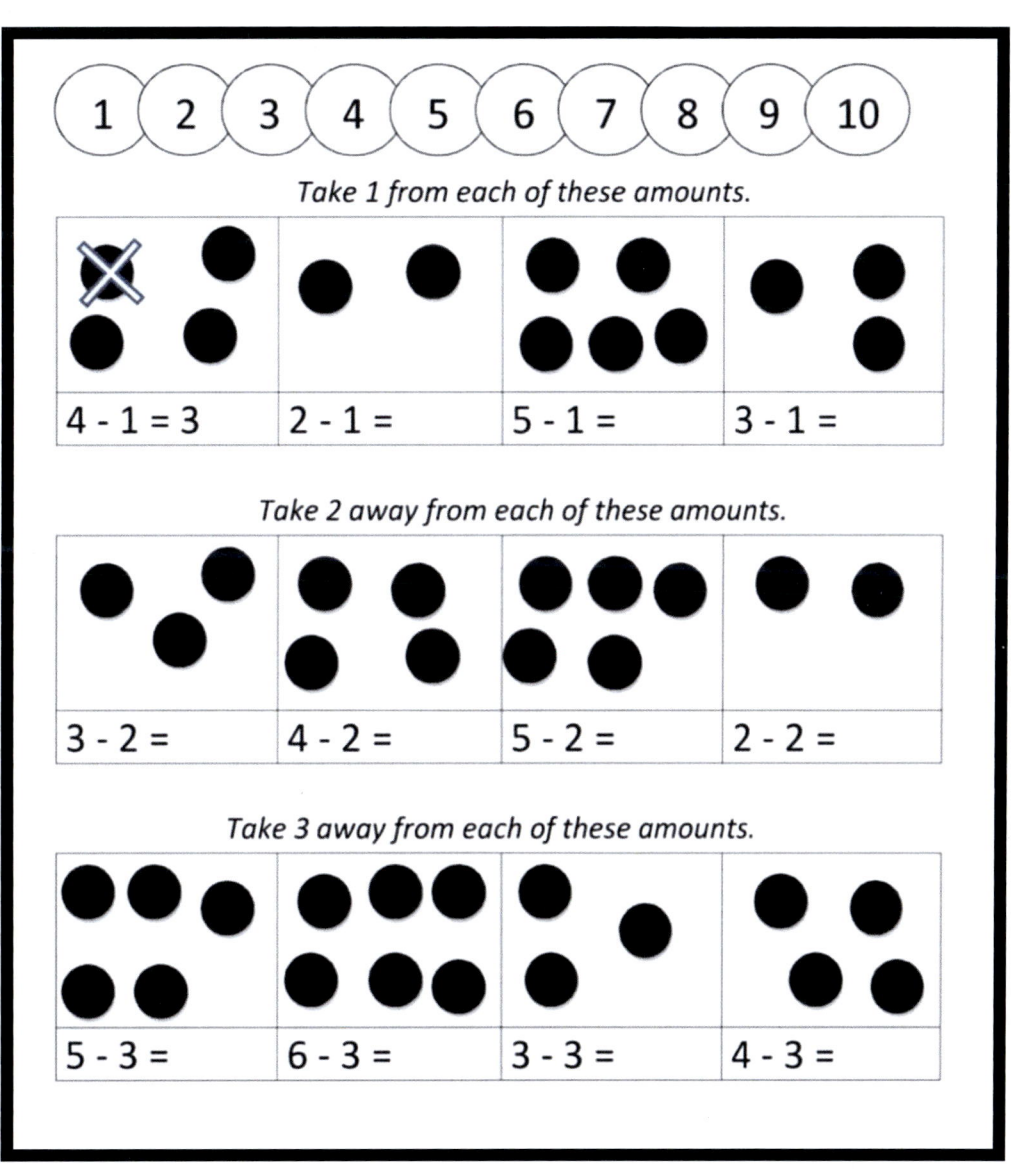

Apple Subtraction

Directions, Solve the subtraction problems by crossing out the numbers to be subtracted. Write the answers on the line

5-2=____

4-3=____

5-4=____

3-2=____

4-2=____

3-3=____

Subtraction

Subtract the numbers and write the answer in the box.

8	4	9
- 5	- 2	- 4

3	7	1 8
- 2	- 3	- 6

1 2	1 7	1 0
- 3	- 9	- 1

Subtraction to 5

Count and subtract.

 3 - 1 = ☐

 5 - 3 = ☐

 4 - 2 = ☐

Count the fingers and subtract the number.

 - 2 = ☐    - 2 = ☐

 - 3 = ☐    - 2 = ☐

 - 1 = ☐    - 4 = ☐

SUBTRACTION

Find how many left in each box and write the correct number.

6 - 2 =

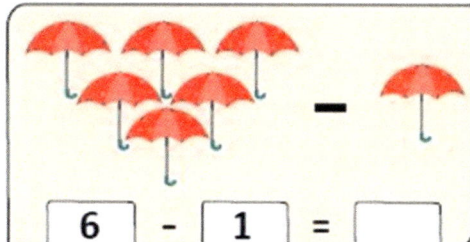
6 - 1 =

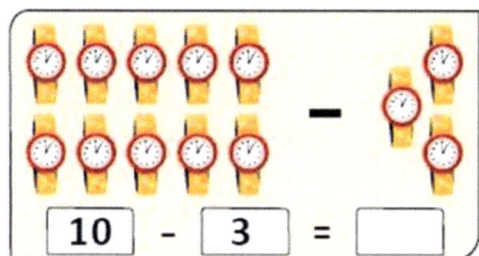
10 - 3 =

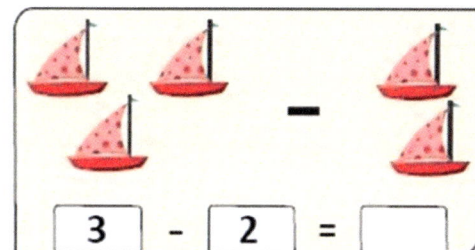
3 - 2 =

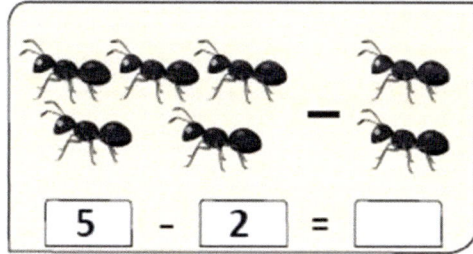
5 - 2 =

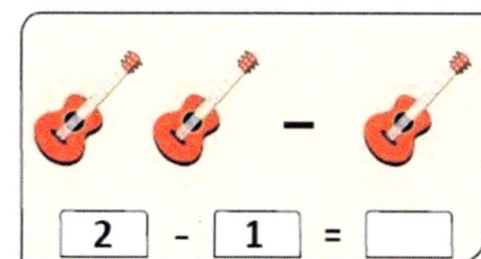
2 - 1 =

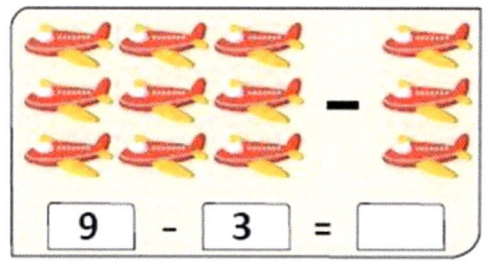
9 - 3 =

4 - 2 =

Keep going

Count the number of dots on each domino and fill in the total.

___ + ___ = ___   ___ + ___ = ___   ___ + ___ = ___

___ + ___ = ___   ___ + ___ = ___   ___ + ___ = ___

___ + ___ = ___   ___ + ___ = ___   ___ + ___ = ___

___ + ___ = ___   ___ + ___ = ___   ___ + ___ = ___

Well done

Made in the USA
Middletown, DE
20 June 2023

32961801R00038